ESPECIALLY FOR:

....

FROM:

....

DATE:

....

The Bible Promise Book®
500 SCRIPTURES
≥for≤
BRAVE BOYS

The Bible Promise Book®
500 SCRIPTURES for BRAVE BOYS

Written and Compiled
by Janice Thompson

BARBOUR kidz
A Division of Barbour Publishing

© 2021 by Barbour Publishing

Print ISBN 978-1-64352-912-7

All rights reserved. No part of this publication may be reproduced or transmitted for commercial purposes, except for brief quotations in printed reviews, without written permission of the publisher.

Churches and other noncommercial interests may reproduce portions of this book without the express written permission of Barbour Publishing, provided that the text does not exceed 500 words or 5 percent of the entire book, whichever is less, and that the text is not material quoted from another publisher. When reproducing text from this book, include the following credit line: "From *The Bible Promise Book®: 500 Scriptures for Brave Boys*, published by Barbour Publishing, Inc. Used by permission."

Scripture quotations are taken from the New Life Version (NLV) copyright © 1969 and 2003 by Barbour Publishing, Inc. All rights reserved.

Published by Barbour Publishing, Inc., 1810 Barbour Drive, Uhrichsville, Ohio 44683, www.barbourbooks.com

Our mission is to inspire the world with the life-changing message of the Bible.

Printed in the United States of America.

000814 0621 BP

CONTENTS

Introduction 9
Be a God Pleaser 11
Character Matters 14
Choices 18
Courage 22
Decisions for the Future 26
Doing What's Right 29
Faith to Move Mountains 32
Family Matters! 36
Forgiven to Forgive 40
Friendships Are Important 44
Girls 47
God Knows 50
God's Heart for the Lost 54
God's Love for You, His Son 58
God's Way 62
Gratitude Is Important 65
Growing into a Godly Man 68
Hard Workers Are Awesome! 72
Healthy and Strong 75
Helping Those in Need 79
Jesus Loves Me 83
Joy for Life's Adventure 87
Kindness 91
Light in the Darkness 95

Make Each Day Count	99
Me, Myself, and I?	103
Neighbors	107
Offense	111
Overcoming	115
Patience	119
Peace	123
Prayer	126
Pride Has to Go!	129
Problems	132
Run the Race	136
School Days	140
Self-Control	143
Serving Others	146
Sneaky Behavior	150
Sports	153
Stand Strong	156
Sticky Situations	160
Superheroes	164
This Is a Test	167
Trusting God	170
Watch Those Words!	173
Wise beyond Your Years	176
Witnessing for Christ	179
Worry Gets You Nowhere	183
You're the Only Boy Like You	187

INTRODUCTION

God's Word is filled with rich and wonderful promises for you, His brave boy. You'll find many of those promises in this book.

Whether you're struggling with fear, self-control, or lack of courage, the scripture selections in this book will remind you of God's promise that He is never far away. No matter what mountains you're facing, you can knock them down with the verses you find here.

If you're in an awesome season where everything's going great, that's fantastic! Use this book to help you build your faith. There's plenty to keep you moving forward in your relationship with Jesus.

Don't ever forget: people will sometimes break their promises, but God never will. If His Word says it, you can count on it!

⋛ BE A GOD PLEASER ⋚

Hey, you! Yes, you! Imagine you're standing at a fork in the road. If you take the road to the right, God will give you a standing ovation; but if you take the road to the left, your friends will think you're super cool. So. . .which road do you take? It's not always easy to take the "right" road, but pleasing God should always be the most important thing! Take that first bold step toward Him, brave boy! He promises to guide you—every step of the way!

1
A man cannot please God unless he has faith. Anyone who comes to God must believe that He is. That one must also know that God gives what is promised to the one who keeps on looking for Him.
HEBREWS 11:6

2
Do you think I am trying to get the favor of men, or of God? If I were still trying to please men, I would not be a servant owned by Christ.
GALATIANS 1:10

3

God has allowed us to be trusted with the Good News. Because of this, we preach it to please God, not man. God tests and proves our hearts.
1 THESSALONIANS 2:4

4

When the ways of a man are pleasing to the Lord, He makes even those who hate him to be at peace with him.
PROVERBS 16:7

5

Those who do what their sinful old selves want to do cannot please God.
ROMANS 8:8

6

Do not act like the sinful people of the world. Let God change your life. First of all, let Him give you a new mind. Then you will know what God wants you to do. And the things you do will be good and pleasing and perfect.
ROMANS 12:2

7

*We will receive from Him whatever we ask
if we obey Him and do what He wants.*
1 John 3:22

8

*Remember to do good and help each other.
Gifts like this please God.*
Hebrews 13:16

9

*So if we stay here on earth or go home to Him,
we always want to please Him.*
2 Corinthians 5:9

10

*Then Peter and the missionaries said,
"We must obey God instead of men!"*
Acts 5:29

⋛ CHARACTER MATTERS ⋚

God wants you to be a young man of great character. But what does *that* mean?...
It means you won't lie—you will be truthful at all times. It also means you can be counted on to follow through when you make a promise. To have godly character means you're like Jesus in the way you talk to people, in the work you do, and in your relationships. Character matters—not just to those around you...but to God.

11

But the Lord said to Samuel, "Do not look at the way he looks on the outside or how tall he is, because I have not chosen him. For the Lord does not look at the things man looks at. A man looks at the outside of a person, but the Lord looks at the heart."
1 Samuel 16:7

12

Do not lie to each other. You have put out of your life your old ways. You have now become a new person and are always learning more about Christ. You are being made more like Christ. He is the One Who made you.
COLOSSIANS 3:9–10

13

Christian brothers, keep your minds thinking about whatever is true, whatever is respected, whatever is right, whatever is pure, whatever can be loved, and whatever is well thought of. If there is anything good and worth giving thanks for, think about these things.
PHILIPPIANS 4:8

14

Do not act like the sinful people of the world. Let God change your life. First of all, let Him give you a new mind. Then you will know what God wants you to do. And the things you do will be good and pleasing and perfect.
ROMANS 12:2

15

My Christian brothers, what good does it do if you say you have faith but do not do things that prove you have faith? Can that kind of faith save you from the punishment of sin?
JAMES 2:14

16

In all things show them how to live by your life and by right teaching. You should be wise in what you say. Then the one who is against you will be ashamed and will not be able to say anything bad about you.
TITUS 2:7–8

17

*Do not let anyone fool you.
Bad people can make those who
want to live good become bad.*
1 CORINTHIANS 15:33

18

A good name is to be chosen instead of many riches. Favor is better than silver and gold.
PROVERBS 22:1

19

Do your best to add holy living to your faith. Then add to this a better understanding. As you have a better understanding, be able to say no when you need to. Do not give up. And as you wait and do not give up, live God-like. As you live God-like, be kind to Christian brothers and love them.
2 PETER 1:5–7

20

Happy is the man who does not walk in the way sinful men tell him to, or stand in the path of sinners, or sit with those who laugh at the truth.
PSALM 1:1

CHOICES

Choices, choices. . .so many choices! Everywhere you look, there are things to choose. Should you have the burger or a pepperoni pizza? Should you skip lunch and eat candy instead? Should you obey your parents—or not? Should you be nice to that kid who's always mean to you? He's a real pain, after all. Should you talk to your friends about Jesus or let someone else do that? As you read the following biblical promises, remember: the choices you make today could have "forever" consequences!

21
"Go in through the narrow door. The door is wide and the road is easy that leads to hell. Many people are going through that door. But the door is narrow and the road is hard that leads to life that lasts forever. Few people are finding it."
MATTHEW 7:13–14

22

*There is a way which looks right to a man,
but its end is the way of death.*
PROVERBS 14:12

23

*The mind of a man plans his way,
but the Lord shows him what to do.*
PROVERBS 16:9

24

*Your ears will hear a word behind you, saying,
"This is the way, walk in it," whenever you
turn to the right or to the left.*
ISAIAH 30:21

25

*Christian brothers, keep your minds thinking
about whatever is true, whatever is respected,
whatever is right, whatever is pure, whatever
can be loved, and whatever is well thought of.
If there is anything good and worth giving
thanks for, think about these things.*
PHILIPPIANS 4:8

26

*There are many plans in a man's heart,
but it is the Lord's plan that will stand.*
PROVERBS 19:21

27

*My son, do not forget my teaching. Let your
heart keep my words. For they will add to you
many days and years of life and peace.*
PROVERBS 3:1–2

28

*If you do not have wisdom, ask God for it.
He is always ready to give it to you and
will never say you are wrong for asking.*
JAMES 1:5

29

*You have never been tempted to sin
in any different way than other people.
God is faithful. He will not allow you to
be tempted more than you can take.
But when you are tempted, He will make a
way for you to keep from falling into sin.*
1 CORINTHIANS 10:13

30

*The way of a fool is right in his own eyes,
but a wise man listens to good teaching.*
PROVERBS 12:15

⋛ COURAGE ⋛

God wants to give you courage
to face life's challenges! You can
be brave, young man. Yes, *you!*

C: Say the word *Can* instead of can't.
O: Obstacle. No obstacle is too big for
   you when God's on your side!
U: Unique. God made you a one-of-a-kind kid!
R: Righteous. It's His righteousness,
   not yours!
A: Apple. You're the apple of His eye.
G: Greatness. That's your destiny!
E: Eternity. You're His. . .forever and ever!
   What a wonderful promise!

31

*The Lord is my rock, and my safe place,
and the One Who takes me out of trouble.
My God is my rock, in Whom I am safe.
He is my safe-covering, my saving
strength, and my strong tower.*
PSALM 18:2

32
"Do not fear, for I am with you. Do not be afraid, for I am your God. I will give you strength, and for sure I will help you. Yes, I will hold you up with My right hand that is right and good."
Isaiah 41:10

33
"For I am the Lord your God Who holds your right hand, and Who says to you, 'Do not be afraid. I will help you.'"
Isaiah 41:13

34
"Do not be afraid of them who kill the body. They are not able to kill the soul. But fear Him Who is able to destroy both soul and body in hell."
Matthew 10:28

35

*"Be strong and have strength of heart.
Do not be afraid or shake with fear because
of them. For the Lord your God is the One
Who goes with you. He will be faithful
to you. He will not leave you alone."*
DEUTERONOMY 31:6

36

*There is no fear in love. Perfect love puts fear
out of our hearts. People have fear when they
are afraid of being punished. The man who
is afraid does not have perfect love.*
1 JOHN 4:18

37

*The Lord is my light and the One Who saves me.
Whom should I fear? The Lord is the strength
of my life. Of whom should I be afraid?*
PSALM 27:1

38

*For God did not give us a spirit of fear.
He gave us a spirit of power and of
love and of a good mind.*
2 Timothy 1:7

39

*Watch and keep awake! Stand true to the Lord.
Keep on acting like men and be strong.*
1 Corinthians 16:13

40

*Then David said to his son Solomon, "Be strong.
Have strength of heart, and do it. Do not be
afraid or troubled, for the Lord God, my God,
is with you. He will not stop helping you.
He will not leave you until all the work
of the house of the Lord is finished."*
1 Chronicles 28:20

DECISIONS FOR THE FUTURE

You've got a lot to think about, brave boy. . . like what kind of man you'll be when you grow up. What sort of job you'll have. Where you'll live. Who you'll marry. How many kids you'll have. That's a *lot* to decide. Aren't you glad you don't have to have it all figured out now? Here's the truth: God will help you make the very best decisions for your life. That means you never have to worry or be afraid of the future. That's a promise for anyone who trusts in Him.

41

Trust in the Lord with all your heart, and do not trust in your own understanding. Agree with Him in all your ways, and He will make your paths straight.
PROVERBS 3:5–6

42

Teach me Your way, O Lord. I will walk in Your truth. May my heart fear Your name.
PSALM 86:11

43

"Do not fear, for I am with you. Do not be afraid, for I am your God. I will give you strength, and for sure I will help you. Yes, I will hold you up with My right hand that is right and good."
ISAIAH 41:10

44

" 'For I know the plans I have for you,' says the Lord, 'plans for well-being and not for trouble, to give you a future and a hope.' "
JEREMIAH 29:11

45

But the one who keeps looking into God's perfect Law and does not forget it will do what it says and be happy as he does it. God's Word makes men free.
JAMES 1:25

46

Trust your work to the Lord, and your plans will work out well.
PROVERBS 16:3

47
"Peace I leave with you. My peace I give to you.
I do not give peace to you as the world gives.
Do not let your hearts be troubled or afraid."
JOHN 14:27

48
Plans go wrong without talking together,
but they will go well when many wise
men talk about what to do.
PROVERBS 15:22

49
The mind of a man plans his way,
but the Lord shows him what to do.
PROVERBS 16:9

50
I am sure that God Who began the good
work in you will keep on working in you
until the day Jesus Christ comes again.
PHILIPPIANS 1:6

⇉ DOING WHAT'S RIGHT ⇇

Sometimes it seems easier to disobey, doesn't it? For example: Dad tells you to sweep the garage floor, but you don't feel like it. . .so you end up playing a video game instead. An hour later, Dad comes into the garage and sees you haven't done a thing. And now you're grounded from video games and stuck in the garage until the floor is clean. It's always better to do the right thing in the first place, for sure! And, even better, God promises to honor your obedience.

51
*"If you love Me,
you will do what I say."*
JOHN 14:15

52
*"Not everyone who says to me,
'Lord, Lord,' will go into the holy nation
of heaven. The one who does the things
My Father in heaven wants him to do
will go into the holy nation of heaven."*
MATTHEW 7:21

53

Jesus said, "The one who loves Me will obey My teaching. My Father will love him. We will come to him and live with him."
JOHN 14:23

54

"And why do you call Me, 'Lord, Lord,' but do not do what I say?"
LUKE 6:46

55

Adam did not obey God, and many people become sinners through him. Christ obeyed God and makes many people right with Himself.
ROMANS 5:19

56

Love means that we should live by obeying His Word. From the beginning He has said in His Word that our hearts should be full of love.
2 JOHN 1:6

57
Obey the Word of God. If you hear only and do not act, you are only fooling yourself.
JAMES 1:22

58
Samuel said, "Is the Lord pleased as much with burnt gifts as He is when He is obeyed? See, it is better to obey than to give gifts. It is better to listen than to give the fat of rams."
1 SAMUEL 15:22

59
"If you are willing and obey, you will eat the best of the land."
ISAIAH 1:19

60
Then Peter and the missionaries said, "We must obey God instead of men!"
ACTS 5:29

FAITH TO MOVE MOUNTAINS

Are you a mountain mover? Maybe you don't even know what that means. God's Word says that problems are like mountains. That kid in school who won't leave you alone? He's a mountain. That math equation you can't seem to solve? Another mountain. Here's the good news: the Bible says that you can speak to the mountains in your life—in the name of Jesus—and they will disappear right before your eyes. What an amazing promise!

61

If you do not have wisdom, ask God for it. He is always ready to give it to you and will never say you are wrong for asking. You must have faith as you ask Him. You must not doubt. Anyone who doubts is like a wave which is pushed around by the sea. Such a man will get nothing from the Lord. The man who has two ways of thinking changes in everything he does.
JAMES 1:5–8

62
Jesus said to them, "Because you have so little faith. For sure, I tell you, if you have faith as a mustard seed, you will say to this mountain, 'Move from here to over there,' and it would move over. You will be able to do anything."
MATTHEW 17:20

63
Now faith is being sure we will get what we hope for. It is being sure of what we cannot see.
HEBREWS 11:1

64
"All things you ask for in prayer, you will receive if you have faith."
MATTHEW 21:22

65

The Lord said, "If your faith was as a mustard seed, you could say to this tree, 'Be pulled out of the ground and planted in the sea,' and it would obey you."
Luke 17:6

66

The followers said to the Lord, "Give us more faith."
Luke 17:5

67

"The Holy Writings say that rivers of living water will flow from the heart of the one who puts his trust in Me."
John 7:38

68
*I have fought a good fight. I have
finished the work I was to do.
I have kept the faith.*
2 TIMOTHY 4:7

69
*"We believe and know You are the Christ.
You are the Son of the Living God."*
JOHN 6:69

70
*A man cannot please God unless he
has faith. Anyone who comes to God
must believe that He is. That one must
also know that God gives what is promised
to the one who keeps on looking for Him.*
HEBREWS 11:6

⋛ FAMILY MATTERS! ⋚

God is so happy when kids and parents love each other and live together peacefully. He wants your family relationships to be positive and joy filled! No matter what you're going through—even if your family is struggling—God can help make things better. That's a promise! Do what's right (love and obey your parents), and then watch as God honors your obedience. Exciting things lie ahead for those who trust and obey His Word!

71
"Honor your father and your mother, so your life may be long in the land the Lord your God gives you."
Exodus 20:12

72
Bring up a child by teaching him the way he should go, and when he is old he will not turn away from it.
Proverbs 22:6

73

Children, obey your parents in everything. The Lord is pleased when you do.
COLOSSIANS 3:20

74

Your wife will be like a vine with much fruit within your house. Your children will be like olive plants around your table.
PSALM 128:3

75

See, children are a gift from the Lord. The children born to us are our special reward. The children of a young man are like arrows in the hand of a soldier. Happy is the man who has many of them. They will not be put to shame when they speak in the gate with those who hate them.
PSALM 127:3–5

76
Anyone who does not take care of his family and those in his house has turned away from the faith. He is worse than a person who has never put his trust in Christ.
1 Timothy 5:8

77
My son, keep the teaching of your father, and do not turn away from the teaching of your mother.
Proverbs 6:20

78
"Honor your father and your mother, as the Lord your God has told you. So your life may be long and it may go well with you in the land the Lord your God gives you."
Deuteronomy 5:16

79

Then Paul spoke the Word of God to him and his family. It was late at night, but the man who watched the prison took Paul and Silas in and washed the places on their bodies where they were hurt. Right then he and his family were baptized. He took Paul and Silas to his house and gave them food. He and all his family were full of joy for having put their trust in God.
Acts 16:32–34

80

I remember your true faith. It is the same faith your grandmother Lois had and your mother Eunice had. I am sure you have that same faith also.
2 Timothy 1:5

FORGIVEN TO FORGIVE

God will never ask you to do something that He isn't willing to do Himself. So when He tells you to forgive others, it's because He's already forgiven you for all your sins. Forgiving those who hurt us isn't easy, but when we choose to do it, amazing things happen. And that's a promise from the Word of God! *You are now set free to forgive, brave boy!*

81
You must be kind to each other. Think of the other person. Forgive other people just as God forgave you because of Christ's death on the cross.
Ephesians 4:32

82
"When you stand to pray, if you have anything against anyone, forgive him. Then your Father in heaven will forgive your sins also."
Mark 11:25

83

If we tell Him our sins, He is faithful and we can depend on Him to forgive us of our sins. He will make our lives clean from all sin.
1 John 1:9

84

Then Peter came to Jesus and said, "Lord, how many times may my brother sin against me and I forgive him, up to seven times?" Jesus said to him, "I tell you, not seven times but seventy times seven!"
Matthew 18:21–22

85

"Do not say what is wrong in other people's lives. Then other people will not say what is wrong in your life. Do not say someone is guilty. Then other people will not say you are guilty. Forgive other people and other people will forgive you."
Luke 6:37

86
"If you do not forgive people their sins, your Father will not forgive your sins."
MATTHEW 6:15

87
Try to understand other people. Forgive each other. If you have something against someone, forgive him. That is the way the Lord forgave you.
COLOSSIANS 3:13

88
Tell your sins to each other. And pray for each other so you may be healed. The prayer from the heart of a man right with God has much power.
JAMES 5:16

89
"I say to you who hear Me, love those
who work against you. Do good
to those who hate you."
LUKE 6:27

90
Because of the blood of Christ, we are
bought and made free from the punishment
of sin. And because of His blood, our sins
are forgiven. His loving-favor to us is so rich.
EPHESIANS 1:7

FRIENDSHIPS ARE IMPORTANT

Where would we be without our friends?
They lift us up when we're feeling down.
They laugh with us when we're feeling goofy.
They give great advice and encourage us to
do our very best. Some friendships are harder
than others; there are a few guys (and girls)
out there who are tougher to get along with.
Choose your friends wisely, and they will help
you to become a better human being.
That, brave boy, is God's promise to you!

91
*A man who has friends must be a friend,
but there is a friend who stays
nearer than a brother.*
PROVERBS 18:24

92
*"No one can have greater love than
to give his life for his friends."*
JOHN 15:13

93
*Iron is made sharp with iron,
and one man is made sharp by a friend.*
PROVERBS 27:17

94
Two are better than one, because they have good pay for their work. For if one of them falls, the other can help him up. But it is hard for the one who falls when there is no one to lift him up.
ECCLESIASTES 4:9–10

95
*Do not let anyone fool you.
Bad people can make those who
want to live good become bad.*
1 CORINTHIANS 15:33

96
So comfort each other and make each other strong as you are already doing.
1 THESSALONIANS 5:11

97

*A bad man spreads trouble.
One who hurts people with bad
talk separates good friends.*
PROVERBS 16:28

98

*He who walks with wise men will be wise, but the
one who walks with fools will be destroyed.*
PROVERBS 13:20

99

*Most of all, have a true love for each other.
Love covers many sins. Be happy to have people
stay for the night and eat with you. God has
given each of you a gift. Use it to help each
other. This will show God's loving-favor.*
1 PETER 4:8–10

100

*"Kindness from a friend should be shown
to a man without hope, or he might turn
away from the fear of the All-powerful."*
JOB 6:14

⋝ GIRLS ⋜

Do you ever wonder why God made girls? They're so different! They have their own way of talking, dressing, and acting. Sometimes you just can't figure them out, so you roll your eyes and ignore them. Here's a fun fact: as you get older, you'll start to care more about girls. That's how God designed you. So it's important to figure out how to treat girls with kindness and tenderness now. The Lord will honor your goodness toward them. That's a promise!

101
And God made man in His own likeness. In the likeness of God He made him. He made both male and female.
GENESIS 1:27

102
Nothing should be done because of pride or thinking about yourself. Think of other people as more important than yourself.
PHILIPPIANS 2:3

103

Do not speak sharp words to an older man. Talk with him as if he were a father. Talk to younger men as brothers. Talk to older women as mothers. Talk to younger women as sisters, keeping yourself pure.
1 Timothy 5:1–2

104

She opens her mouth with wisdom. The teaching of kindness is on her tongue.
Proverbs 31:26

105

For You made the parts inside me. You put me together inside my mother.
Psalm 139:13

106

Pleasing ways lie and beauty comes to nothing, but a woman who fears the Lord will be praised.
Proverbs 31:30

107

*O man, He has told you what is good.
What does the Lord ask of you but to
do what is fair and to love kindness,
and to walk without pride with your God?*
MICAH 6:8

108

*Her clothes are strength and honor.
She is full of joy about the future.*
PROVERBS 31:25

109

*Because of this, we should do good to
everyone. For sure, we should do good
to those who belong to Christ.*
GALATIANS 6:10

110

*"I give you a new Law. You are to love each other.
You must love each other as I have loved you."*
JOHN 13:34

⦃ GOD KNOWS ⦄

Does it seem strange that God knows what you're going to do before you do it? He even knows what you're going to say before you say it. Crazy, right?... But it's true! God is omniscient. That means He knows absolutely *everything*. And because He knows you best (and loves you most), you can trust Him with everything. He already sees and knows what you're going through, and best of all...He cares. What an amazing promise!

111
Great is our Lord, and great in power. His understanding has no end.
PSALM 147:5

112
Our heart may say that we have done wrong. But remember, God is greater than our heart. He knows everything.
1 JOHN 3:20

113

"Before I started to put you together in your mother, I knew you. Before you were born, I set you apart as holy. I chose you to speak to the nations for Me."
JEREMIAH 1:5

114

The eyes of the Lord are in every place, watching the bad and the good.
PROVERBS 15:3

115

Have you not known? Have you not heard? The God Who lives forever is the Lord, the One Who made the ends of the earth. He will not become weak or tired. His understanding is too great for us to begin to know.
ISAIAH 40:28

116

"Can a man hide himself in secret places so that I cannot see him?" says the Lord. "Do I not fill heaven and earth?" says the Lord.
JEREMIAH 23:24

117

He knows the number of the stars. He gives names to all of them. Great is our Lord, and great in power. His understanding has no end.
PSALM 147:4–5

118

*Even before I speak a word,
O Lord, You know it all.*
PSALM 139:4

119

"When you pray, do not say the same thing over and over again making long prayers like the people who do not know God. They think they are heard because their prayers are long. Do not be like them. Your Father knows what you need before you ask Him."
MATTHEW 6:7–8

120

"Are not two small birds sold for a very small piece of money? And yet not one of the birds falls to the earth without your Father knowing it."
MATTHEW 10:29

GOD'S HEART FOR THE LOST

The Bible calls those who don't yet know Jesus "lost." But that's only because they don't know Him yet. Here's the good news: with your help, they can come to know Him. So, how does God feel about "lost" people? Does He love them as much as He loves believers? The truth is, the Lord cares about all His kids, lost and saved! And He wants you to treat all people with such kindness that they come to realize His love because of your example.

121

"What if a woman has ten silver pieces of money and loses one of them? Does she not light a lamp and sweep the floor and look until she finds it? When she finds it, she calls her friends and neighbors together. She says to them, 'Be happy with me. I have found the piece of money I had lost.' I tell you, it is the same way among the angels of God. If one sinner is sorry for his sins and turns from them, the angels are very happy."
Luke 15:8–10

122

The Lord is not slow about keeping His promise as some people think. He is waiting for you. The Lord does not want any person to be punished forever. He wants all people to be sorry for their sins and turn from them.
2 PETER 3:9

123

For by His loving-favor you have been saved from the punishment of sin through faith. It is not by anything you have done. It is a gift of God. It is not given to you because you worked for it. If you could work for it, you would be proud.
EPHESIANS 2:8–9

124

"I tell you, there will be more joy in heaven because of one sinner who is sorry for his sins and turns from them, than for ninety-nine people right with God who do not have sins to be sorry for."
LUKE 15:7

125

"I am the Good Shepherd. The Good Shepherd gives His life for the sheep."
JOHN 10:11

126

Jesus sent out these twelve followers. He told them to go, saying, "Stay away from people who are not Jews. And do not go to any town in the country of Samaria. But go to the Jewish people who are lost."
MATTHEW 10:5–6

127

"For God so loved the world that He gave His only Son. Whoever puts his trust in God's Son will not be lost but will have life that lasts forever."
JOHN 3:16

128
You were like lost sheep. But now you have come back to Him Who is your Shepherd and the One Who cares for your soul.
1 P‍eter 2:25

129
"For the Son of Man came to look for and to save from the punishment of sin those who are lost."
Luke 19:10

130
For the Lord God says, "I Myself will look for My sheep and find them."
Ezekiel 34:11

GOD'S LOVE FOR YOU, HIS SON

You might not like to talk about love—
at least not the mushy kind. But there's
one kind of love you need to know about:
God's love for you, His son. It's true! His love
for you is deeper than the deepest ocean,
wider than the widest desert, and higher than
the highest mountain. And there's nothing
you can do to change that. What a remarkable
promise! If you ever start to wonder, *Does God
really love me, or does the Bible just say that?*
you will find the answer here: He loves you so
much that He sent His Son, Jesus, to die for
your sins. Talk about amazing love!

131

*"For God so loved the world that
He gave His only Son. Whoever puts
his trust in God's Son will not be lost
but will have life that lasts forever."*
JOHN 3:16

132

"The Lord your God is with you, a Powerful One Who wins the battle. He will have much joy over you. With His love He will give you new life. He will have joy over you with loud singing."
Zephaniah 3:17

133

See what great love the Father has for us that He would call us His children. And that is what we are. For this reason the people of the world do not know who we are because they did not know Him.
1 John 3:1

134

For I know that nothing can keep us from the love of God. Death cannot! Life cannot! Angels cannot! Leaders cannot! Any other power cannot! Hard things now or in the future cannot!
Romans 8:38

135

I have been put up on the cross to die with Christ. I no longer live. Christ lives in me. The life I now live in this body, I live by putting my trust in the Son of God. He was the One Who loved me and gave Himself for me.
GALATIANS 2:20

136

*We love Him because
He loved us first.*
1 JOHN 4:19

137

*But You, O Lord, are a God full of love
and pity. You are slow to anger and
rich in loving-kindness and truth.*
PSALM 86:15

138

The Lord came to us from far away, saying, "I have loved you with a love that lasts forever. So I have helped you come to Me with loving-kindness."
JEREMIAH 31:3

139

Give thanks to the God of heaven, for His loving-kindness lasts forever.
PSALM 136:26

140

My lips will praise You because Your loving-kindness is better than life.
PSALM 63:3

⋛ GOD'S WAY ⋛

You can't always figure out what God's up to, can you? Many times, things happen that seem unfair or confusing. But the Bible promises that the Lord is always ready to turn something bad into something good. (As some people like to say, He can turn a test into a testimony!) So, hang on during the tough times and remember this: His ways are higher than yours. And He loves you—which means He's looking out for you, even when bad things happen.

141

"For My thoughts are not your thoughts, and My ways are not your ways," says the Lord. "For as the heavens are higher than the earth, so are My ways higher than your ways, and My thoughts than your thoughts."
ISAIAH 55:8–9

142

Teach me Your way, O Lord. I will walk in Your truth. May my heart fear Your name.
PSALM 86:11

143

*God's riches are so great! The things
He knows and His wisdom are so deep!
No one can understand His thoughts.
No one can understand His ways.*
ROMANS 11:33

144

*There is a way which looks right to a man,
but its end is the way of death.*
PROVERBS 14:12

145

*Many people will come and say, "Come,
let us go up to the mountain of the Lord,
to the house of the God of Jacob. Then He will
teach us about His ways, that we may walk in
His paths. For the Law will go out from Zion,
and the Word of the Lord from Jerusalem."*
ISAIAH 2:3

146

*O Lord, I know that a man's way is not known by
himself. It is not in man to lead his own steps.*
JEREMIAH 10:23

147
Whoever is wise, let him understand these things and know them. For the ways of the Lord are right, and those who are right and good will follow them, but sinners will not follow them.
HOSEA 14:9

148
He leads those without pride into what is right, and teaches them His way.
PSALM 25:9

149
*Show me Your ways, O Lord.
Teach me Your paths.*
PSALM 25:4

150
Trust in the Lord with all your heart, and do not trust in your own understanding.
PROVERBS 3:5

GRATITUDE IS IMPORTANT

God loves it when you come to Him with a heart of gratitude. It brings Him great joy to know that you're thankful for all He's given you—your family, your home, your friends, even that pesky sibling! Remember, all good gifts come from the Lord. You don't deserve any of it; but in His Word He promises to lavish (pour) it out on you, simply because He adores you. So, show Him how grateful you are, brave boy! Today. . .give thanks!

151
In everything give thanks. This is what God wants you to do because of Christ Jesus.
1 THESSALONIANS 5:18

152
Whatever you say or do, do it in the name of the Lord Jesus. Give thanks to God the Father through the Lord Jesus.
COLOSSIANS 3:17

153

*Give thanks to the Lord, for He is good,
for His loving-kindness lasts forever.*
PSALM 136:1

154

*Let the peace of Christ have power
over your hearts. You were chosen as
a part of His body. Always be thankful.*
COLOSSIANS 3:15

155

*Since we have received a holy nation that cannot
be moved, let us be thankful. Let us please God
and worship Him with honor and fear.*
HEBREWS 12:28

156

*Since then, I always give thanks
for you and pray for you.*
EPHESIANS 1:16

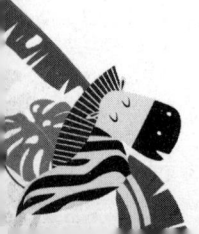

157
*Give thanks to the Lord for He is good!
His loving-kindness lasts forever!*
Psalm 107:1

158
*"He who gives a gift of thanks honors Me.
And to him who makes his way right, I will
show him the saving power of God."*
Psalm 50:23

159
*You are my God and I will give You thanks.
You are my God and I will praise You.
Give thanks to the Lord, for He is good.
His loving-kindness lasts forever.*
Psalm 118:28–29

160
*Let us give thanks all the time to God through
Jesus Christ. Our gift to Him is to give thanks.
Our lips should always give thanks to His name.*
Hebrews 13:15

GROWING INTO A GODLY MAN

God has great plans for you, brave boy. Maybe you wonder, *What plans? He hasn't shown me anything!* That's one of the coolest things about God. . .He *loves* surprises. And boy, does He have some fantastic surprises in mind for you. As you get older, you're going to meet people, go places, and do things you never dreamed. He's going to grow you into a godly man who will make a difference in this world. Begin to pray now. Speak these words, "Lord, have Your way! Use me, I pray! Amen."

161

" 'For I know the plans I have for you,' says the Lord, 'plans for well-being and not for trouble, to give you a future and a hope.' "
JEREMIAH 29:11

162
There are many plans in a man's heart, but it is the Lord's plan that will stand.
PROVERBS 19:21

163
"Before I started to put you together in your mother, I knew you. Before you were born, I set you apart as holy. I chose you to speak to the nations for Me."
Jeremiah 1:5

164
We know that God makes all things work together for the good of those who love Him and are chosen to be a part of His plan.
ROMANS 8:28

165

Trust in the Lord with all your heart, and do not trust in your own understanding. Agree with Him in all your ways, and He will make your paths straight.
PROVERBS 3:5–6

166

"I know that You can do all things. Nothing can put a stop to Your plans."
JOB 42:2

167

I will show you and teach you in the way you should go. I will tell you what to do with My eye upon you.
PSALM 32:8

168
*The mind of a man plans his way,
but the Lord shows him what to do.*
PROVERBS 16:9

169
*I am sure that God Who began the good
work in you will keep on working in you
until the day Jesus Christ comes again.*
PHILIPPIANS 1:6

170
*He is working in you. God is helping
you obey Him. God is doing what
He wants done in you.*
PHILIPPIANS 2:13

HARD WORKERS ARE AWESOME!

Would you call yourself a hard worker? Sure, you do your schoolwork (and even tackle your homework), but do you always follow through when Mom says things like, "Get in there and clean your room, son!"? Maybe not. God loves it when His guys do the work—even the hard work. Loading the dishwasher or cleaning up your baby brother's toys might not sound like fun—but when you do those things, you're proving to God that you're obedient. So, get to it, young man! You've got work to do!

171
Whatever work you do, do it with all your heart. Do it for the Lord and not for men.
COLOSSIANS 3:23

172
Some good comes from all work. Nothing but talk leads only to being poor.
PROVERBS 14:23

173

*Trust your work to the Lord,
and your plans will work out well.*
PROVERBS 16:3

174

*So if you eat or drink or whatever
you do, do everything to honor God.*
1 CORINTHIANS 10:31

175

*Do your best to live a quiet life. Learn to do
your own work well. We told you about this
before. By doing this, you will be respected by
those who are not Christians. Then you will not
be in need and others will not have to help you.*
1 THESSALONIANS 4:11–12

176

*Do not let yourselves get tired of doing good.
If we do not give up, we will get what is
coming to us at the right time.*
GALATIANS 6:9

177

*He who works his land will have all the
bread he needs, but he who follows
what is of no worth has no wisdom.*
PROVERBS 12:11

178

*Let the favor of the Lord our God be upon us.
And make the work of our hands stand strong.
Yes, make the work of our hands stand strong.*
PSALM 90:17

179

*Do you see a man who is good at his work?
He will stand in front of kings. He will not
stand in front of men who are not important.*
PROVERBS 22:29

180

*The Lord will finish the work He started for me.
O Lord, Your loving-kindness lasts forever.
Do not turn away from the works of Your hands.*
PSALM 138:8

HEALTHY AND STRONG

The Bible says that Jesus went from place to place, healing the sick. He never turned anyone away, no matter who they were or what they'd done. Here's a fun fact: God is still in the healing business. It's true! You'll find that promise in His Word. He can heal diseases, but He can also heal broken hearts and fix broken relationships. If you're in need of healing, go to Him and ask. He's excited to hear from you and wants to give you a healthy life.

181

Dear friend, I pray that you are doing well in every way. I pray that your body is strong and well even as your soul is.
3 John 1:2

182

A glad heart is good medicine, but a broken spirit dries up the bones.
Proverbs 17:22

183

He said, "Listen well to the voice of the Lord your God. Do what is right in His eyes. Listen to what He tells you, and obey all His Laws. If you do this, I will put none of the diseases on you which I have put on the Egyptians. For I am the Lord Who heals you."
EXODUS 15:26

184

Do not be wise in your own eyes. Fear the Lord and turn away from what is sinful. It will be healing to your body and medicine to your bones.
PROVERBS 3:7–8

185

Pleasing words are like honey. They are sweet to the soul and healing to the bones.
PROVERBS 16:24

186

"Serve the Lord your God and He will give you bread and water. And I will take sickness from among you."
Exodus 23:25

187

He heals those who have a broken heart. He heals their sorrows.
Psalm 147:3

188

"For I will heal you. I will heal you where you have been hurt," says the Lord, "because they have said that you are not wanted. They have said, 'It is Zion. No one cares for her.' "
Jeremiah 30:17

189

But He was hurt for our wrong-doing. He was crushed for our sins. He was punished so we would have peace. He was beaten so we would be healed.
Isaiah 53:5

190

He carried our sins in His own body when He died on a cross. In doing this, we may be dead to sin and alive to all that is right and good. His wounds have healed you!
1 Peter 2:24

HELPING THOSE IN NEED

This big, wide world is filled with people in need. Some need food. Some need clothes and shoes. Here's the cool thing: *you* can be the hands and feet of Jesus by helping those in need. You can donate food to your church's food pantry, donate clothes you've outgrown, and even work (with your parents) at a homeless shelter. No matter how you decide to help, do so with a smile on your face and the love of Jesus in your heart. He promises to bless you as you bless others.

191

"For I was hungry and you gave Me food to eat. I was thirsty and you gave Me water to drink. I was a stranger and you gave Me a room. I had no clothes and you gave Me clothes to wear. I was sick and you cared for Me. I was in prison and you came to see Me."
MATTHEW 25:35–36

192

"If you see your brother's donkey or his ox fallen down by the road, do not pretend that you do not see them. Be sure to help him lift them up again."
DEUTERONOMY 22:4

193

Help each other in troubles and problems. This is the kind of law Christ asks us to obey.
GALATIANS 6:2

194

"Sell what you have and give the money to poor people. Have money-bags for yourselves that will never wear out. These money-bags are riches in heaven that will always be there. No robber can take them and no bugs can eat them there."
LUKE 12:33

195

"In every way I showed you that by working hard like this we can help those who are weak. We must remember what the Lord Jesus said, 'We are more happy when we give than when we receive.'"
ACTS 20:35

196

"The poor will always be in the land. So I tell you to be free in giving to your brother, to those in need, and to the poor in your land."
DEUTERONOMY 15:11

197

He who shows kindness to a poor man gives to the Lord and He will pay him in return for his good act.
PROVERBS 19:17

198

*He who gives much will be honored,
for he gives some of his food to the poor.*
PROVERBS 22:9

199

*What if a person has enough money to live
on and sees his brother in need of food
and clothing? If he does not help him,
how can the love of God be in him?*
1 JOHN 3:17

200

*He who makes it hard for the poor brings
shame to his Maker, but he who shows
loving-favor to those in need honors Him.*
PROVERBS 14:31

⋛ Jesus Loves Me ⋚

"Jesus loves me, this I know"... These words are so much more than a child's song—they are truth that will guide you and give you joy, peace, and strength for all your life. And it's a biblical promise! Nothing you can ever do will stop Jesus from loving you. He adores you—on good days and bad. So, why not share that love with others today! Ready, set. . .go!

201
"For God so loved the world that He gave His only Son. Whoever puts his trust in God's Son will not be lost but will have life that lasts forever."
John 3:16

202
We have come to know and believe the love God has for us. God is love. If you live in love, you live by the help of God and God lives in you.
1 John 4:16

203

But God had so much loving-kindness. He loved us with such a great love. Even when we were dead because of our sins, He made us alive by what Christ did for us. You have been saved from the punishment of sin by His loving-favor.
EPHESIANS 2:4–5

204

"No one can have greater love than to give his life for his friends."
JOHN 15:13

205

But God showed His love to us. While we were still sinners, Christ died for us.
ROMANS 5:8

206
See what great love the Father has for us that He would call us His children. And that is what we are. For this reason the people of the world do not know who we are because they did not know Him.
1 JOHN 3:1

207
We love Him because He loved us first.
1 JOHN 4:19

208
But You, O Lord, are a God full of love and pity. You are slow to anger and rich in loving-kindness and truth.
PSALM 86:15

209

"The Lord your God is with you, a Powerful One Who wins the battle. He will have much joy over you. With His love He will give you new life. He will have joy over you with loud singing."
ZEPHANIAH 3:17

210

The Lord came to us from far away, saying, "I have loved you with a love that lasts forever. So I have helped you come to Me with loving-kindness."
JEREMIAH 31:3

JOY FOR LIFE'S ADVENTURE

Would people describe you as joyful and filled with life? That's good! God wants His guys to overflow with joy. Of course, life isn't always easy. You will sometimes have struggles. There will still be pain and heartache from time to time. But even in the middle of all of that, if your heart is filled with the kind of joy that only Jesus can bring, He promises to bring you through with a smile on your face.

211
Our hope comes from God. May He fill you with joy and peace because of your trust in Him. May your hope grow stronger by the power of the Holy Spirit.
ROMANS 15:13

212
Be full of joy always because you belong to the Lord. Again I say, be full of joy!
PHILIPPIANS 4:4

213
My Christian brothers, you should be happy when you have all kinds of tests.
JAMES 1:2

214
"Until now you have not asked for anything in My name. Ask and you will receive. Then your joy will be full."
JOHN 16:24

215
A glad heart is good medicine, but a broken spirit dries up the bones.
PROVERBS 17:22

216
You will show me the way of life. Being with You is to be full of joy. In Your right hand there is happiness forever.
Psalm 16:11

217
This is the day that the Lord has made. Let us be full of joy and be glad in it.
Psalm 118:24

218
For His anger lasts only a short time. But His favor is for life. Crying may last for a night, but joy comes with the new day.
Psalm 30:5

219
*"I have told you these things
so My joy may be in you
and your joy may be full."*
John 15:11

220
*Show your happiness, all peoples!
Call out to God with the voice of joy!*
Psalm 47:1

⋛ KINDNESS ⋚

Do you show kindness to others?
Maybe you have to pause and think about
that. Some people are easier to treat with
kindness, after all. But God wants you to be
kind to everyone. That boy who's mean to you?
Respond with kindness. That big sister who
annoys you? Her too. It might seem impossible,
but as you practice kindness, you'll get better
at it. And guess what? It's contagious!
So, let your kindness show, brave boy!

221
*You must be kind to each other. Think of
the other person. Forgive other people
just as God forgave you because of
Christ's death on the cross.*
EPHESIANS 4:32

222
*The man who shows loving-kindness
does himself good, but the man
without pity hurts himself.*
PROVERBS 11:17

223

God has chosen you. You are holy and loved by Him. Because of this, your new life should be full of loving-pity. You should be kind to others and have no pride. Be gentle and be willing to wait for others.
COLOSSIANS 3:12

224

She opens her mouth with wisdom. The teaching of kindness is on her tongue.
PROVERBS 31:26

225

O man, He has told you what is good. What does the Lord ask of you but to do what is fair and to love kindness, and to walk without pride with your God?
MICAH 6:8

226
Because of this, we should do good to everyone. For sure, we should do good to those who belong to Christ.
GALATIANS 6:10

227
But the fruit that comes from having the Holy Spirit in our lives is: love, joy, peace, not giving up, being kind, being good, having faith.
GALATIANS 5:22

228
We see how kind God is. It shows how hard He is also. He is hard on those who fall away. But He is kind to you if you keep on trusting Him. If you do not, He will cut you off.
ROMANS 11:22

229

Love does not give up. Love is kind. Love is not jealous. Love does not put itself up as being important. Love has no pride. Love does not do the wrong thing. Love never thinks of itself. Love does not get angry. Love does not remember the suffering that comes from being hurt by someone.
1 Corinthians 13:4–5

230

He who follows what is right and loving and kind finds life, right-standing with God and honor.
Proverbs 21:21

LIGHT IN THE DARKNESS

Have you ever been in a very dark room—where you couldn't see a thing? It's kind of scary, isn't it? People across this world are walking in darkness, and they don't even realize it. They haven't seen the light of Jesus yet. Will you let Him shine through you, so that others can see and come to know Him? He promises to use you if you ask. It's the greatest thing in the world to lead others to their Savior by letting your light shine!

231

Jesus spoke to all the people, saying, "I am the Light of the world. Anyone who follows Me will not walk in darkness. He will have the Light of Life."
JOHN 8:12

232

The Light shines in the darkness. The darkness has never been able to put out the Light.
JOHN 1:5

233
*Your Word is a lamp to my
feet and a light to my path.*
PSALM 119:105

234
*"Let your light shine in front of men.
Then they will see the good things you do
and will honor your Father Who is in heaven."*
MATTHEW 5:16

235
*If we live in the light as He is in the light,
we share what we have in God with each
other. And the blood of Jesus Christ,
His Son, makes our lives clean from all sin.*
1 JOHN 1:7

236
This is what we heard Him tell us. We are passing it on to you. God is light. There is no darkness in Him.
1 John 1:5

237
At one time you lived in darkness. Now you are living in the light that comes from the Lord. Live as children who have the light of the Lord in them.
Ephesians 5:8

238
You are the light of the world. You cannot hide a city that is on a mountain.
Matthew 5:14

239

But you are a chosen group of people. You are the King's religious leaders. You are a holy nation. You belong to God. He has done this for you so you can tell others how God has called you out of darkness into His great light.
1 Peter 2:9

240

The Lord is my light and the One Who saves me. Whom should I fear? The Lord is the strength of my life. Of whom should I be afraid?
Psalm 27:1

Make Each Day Count

How do you spend your days? Do you play? Do schoolwork? Eat meals with your family? Clean your room? Sleep? Start all over again the next day? God wants you to be wise about how you spend your time! In the middle of your busyness, don't forget to make time for Him. God promises that if you pray and read your Bible, you will grow in your faith. . . so make every day count!

241

Teach us to understand how many days we have. Then we will have a heart of wisdom to give You.
Psalm 90:12

242

So be careful how you live. Live as men who are wise and not foolish. Make the best use of your time. These are sinful days. Do not be foolish. Understand what the Lord wants you to do.
Ephesians 5:15–17

243
Be wise in the way you live around those who are not Christians. Make good use of your time.
COLOSSIANS 4:5

244
We do not look at the things that can be seen. We look at the things that cannot be seen. The things that can be seen will come to an end. But the things that cannot be seen will last forever.
2 CORINTHIANS 4:18

245
The mind of a man plans his way, but the Lord shows him what to do.
PROVERBS 16:9

246
We are sure of this. We know that while we are at home in this body we are not with the Lord. Our life is lived by faith. We do not live by what we see in front of us.
2 Corinthians 5:6–7

247
Do not talk much about tomorrow, for you do not know what a day will bring.
Proverbs 27:1

248
Listen! You who say, "Today or tomorrow we will go to this city and stay a year and make money." You do not know about tomorrow. What is your life? It is like fog. You see it and soon it is gone.
James 4:13–14

249

He has made everything beautiful in its time. He has put thoughts of the forever in man's mind, yet man cannot understand the work God has done from the beginning to the end.
ECCLESIASTES 3:11

250

As for me, I will call on God and the Lord will save me. I will cry out and complain in the evening and morning and noon, and He will hear my voice.
PSALM 55:16–17

⋛ ME, MYSELF, AND I? ⋚

"I want what I want, and I want it now!" Have you ever been guilty of using (or thinking) those words? Most human beings are a little selfish. It's hard not to put your own needs first. But God wants you to let go of that "me, myself, and I" attitude and begin to love others as you love yourself. This can only happen if you love Him most of all. When you do, He promises to show you how to best love and serve others.

251
What if a person has enough money to live on and sees his brother in need of food and clothing? If he does not help him, how can the love of God be in him?
1 JOHN 3:17

252
Do not work only for your own good. Think of what you can do for others.
1 CORINTHIANS 10:24

253

Nothing should be done because of pride or thinking about yourself. Think of other people as more important than yourself. Do not always be thinking about your own plans only. Be happy to know what other people are doing.
PHILIPPIANS 2:3–4

254

Love does not do the wrong thing. Love never thinks of itself. Love does not get angry. Love does not remember the suffering that comes from being hurt by someone.
1 CORINTHIANS 13:5

255

Help each other in troubles and problems. This is the kind of law Christ asks us to obey.
GALATIANS 6:2

256

We who have strong faith should help those who are weak. We should not live to please ourselves. Each of us should live to please his neighbor. This will help him grow in faith. Even Christ did not please Himself. The Holy Writings say, "The sharp words spoken against you fell on Me."
ROMANS 15:1–3

257

Remember to do good and help each other. Gifts like this please God.
HEBREWS 13:16

258

Those who love only themselves and do not obey the truth, but do what is wrong, will be punished by God. His anger will be on them.
ROMANS 2:8

259

Then Jesus said to them all, "If anyone wants to follow Me, he must give up himself and his own desires. He must take up his cross everyday and follow Me."
LUKE 9:23

260

What if a Christian does not have clothes or food? And one of you says to him, "Goodbye, keep yourself warm and eat well." But if you do not give him what he needs, how does that help him? A faith that does not do things is a dead faith.
JAMES 2:15–17

⋛ NEIGHBORS ⋚

"Who is my neighbor?" one man asked Jesus. Our Savior responded by telling him a story about a guy who cared for a stranger who had been injured. According to God, everyone is our neighbor! So, when He says, "Love your neighbor," He's not just talking about the family next door. Jesus wants you to treat all the people you meet just as you would treat your next-door neighbor—with love, kindness, and generosity.

261
"The second Law is this: 'You must love your neighbor as yourself.' No other Law is greater than these."
Mark 12:31

262
You do well when you obey the Holy Writings which say, "You must love your neighbor as you love yourself."
James 2:8

263
*Each of us should live to please his neighbor.
This will help him grow in faith.*
ROMANS 15:2

264
*You obey the whole Law when
you do this one thing, "Love your
neighbor as you love yourself."*
GALATIANS 5:14

265
*Do not plan for your neighbor
to be hurt, while he trusts you
enough to live beside you.*
PROVERBS 3:29

266
Because of this, we should do good to everyone. For sure, we should do good to those who belong to Christ.
GALATIANS 6:10

267
Anyone who loves his neighbor will do no wrong to him. You keep the Law with love.
ROMANS 13:10

268
"Do for other people what you would like to have them do for you."
LUKE 6:31

269

The man said, "You must love the Lord your God with all your heart. You must love Him with all your soul. You must love Him with all your strength. You must love Him with all your mind. You must love your neighbor as you love yourself."
LUKE 10:27

270

"Do not tell a lie about your neighbor."
EXODUS 20:16

⸝ OFFENSE ⸜

"I'm so offended!" Have you ever used those words? It's easy to get your feelings hurt when people say mean things or leave you out. But God doesn't want you to be offended. He wants you to forgive the person who hurt you and move on. When you live like this, He promises to give you peace in your heart. You'll also build lasting friendships while you're shining the light of Jesus for all to see.

271
A man's understanding makes him slow to anger. It is to his honor to forgive and forget a wrong done to him.
PROVERBS 19:11

272
A brother who has been hurt in his spirit is harder to be won than a strong city, and arguing is like the iron gates of a king's house.
PROVERBS 18:19

273

If men speak bad of you because you are a Christian, you will be happy because the Spirit of shining-greatness and of God is in you.
1 Peter 4:14

274

Live and work without pride. Be gentle and kind. Do not be hard on others. Let love keep you from doing that. Work hard to live together as one by the help of the Holy Spirit. Then there will be peace.
Ephesians 4:2–3

275

My Christian brothers, you know everyone should listen much and speak little. He should be slow to become angry.
James 1:19

276

A servant owned by God must not make trouble. He must be kind to everyone. He must be able to teach. He must be willing to suffer when hurt for doing good.
2 Timothy 2:24

277

"You are happy when men hate you and do not want you around and put shame on you because you trust in Me. Be glad in that day. Be full of joy for your reward is much in heaven. Their fathers did these things to the early preachers."
Luke 6:22–23

278

The anger of a fool is known at once, but a wise man does not speak when he is spoken against.
Proverbs 12:16

279
"Watch yourselves! If your brother sins, speak sharp words to him. If he is sorry and turns from his sin, forgive him. What if he sins against you seven times in one day? If he comes to you and says he is sorry and turns from his sin, forgive him."
Luke 17:3–4

280
Whoever hits you on one side of the face, turn so he can hit the other side also. Whoever takes your coat, give him your shirt also.
Luke 6:29

⦂ OVERCOMING ⦂

What does it mean to be an overcomer? Does it mean everything goes your way and you will win every battle? Not at all! If anyone knew what it was like to be an overcomer, it was Jesus. He's got the best battle record ever! To be like Him, you simply have to step out in faith, no matter what life throws your way. Every problem you face will be resolved in God's way and God's time if you just trust in Him. That's a promise you can take to the bank!

281

"I have told you these things so you may have peace in Me. In the world you will have much trouble. But take hope! I have power over the world!"
JOHN 16:33

282

I can do all things because Christ gives me the strength.
PHILIPPIANS 4:13

283
Every child of God has power over the sins of the world. The way we have power over the sins of the world is by our faith. Who could have power over the world except by believing that Jesus is the Son of God?
1 JOHN 5:4–5

284
But we have power over all these things through Jesus Who loves us so much.
ROMANS 8:37

285
"He who has power and wins will receive these things. I will be his God and he will be My son."
REVELATION 21:7

286

But God is the One Who gives us power over sin through Jesus Christ our Lord. We give thanks to Him for this.
1 CORINTHIANS 15:57

287

"I will allow the one who has power and wins to sit with Me on My throne, as I also had power and won and sat down with My Father on His throne."
REVELATION 3:21

288

The Lord is my strength and my safe cover. My heart trusts in Him, and I am helped. So my heart is full of joy. I will thank Him with my song.
PSALM 28:7

289

*The Lord is my light and the One
Who saves me. Whom should I fear?
The Lord is the strength of my life.
Of whom should I be afraid?*
PSALM 27:1

290

*Do not worry. Learn to pray about everything.
Give thanks to God as you ask Him for what you
need. The peace of God is much greater than the
human mind can understand. This peace will keep
your hearts and minds through Christ Jesus.*
PHILIPPIANS 4:6–7

⋛ PATIENCE ⋚

Want a burger? Drive through a fast-food restaurant. Need to eat quickly at home? Pop something in the microwave. These days no one wants to wait for anything. Maybe you're the same. You have a hard time waiting for Christmas. Or birthdays. Or for someone you love to do the right thing. God knows what it's like to wait. He waits a long time for some of His kids to do the right thing too. Be patient, brave boy! God's Word promises that your patience will be rewarded if you don't give up.

291

Be happy in your hope. Do not give up when trouble comes. Do not let anything stop you from praying.
ROMANS 12:12

292

Do not let yourselves get tired of doing good. If we do not give up, we will get what is coming to us at the right time.
GALATIANS 6:9

293
*But if we hope for something
we do not yet see, we must
learn how to wait for it.*
ROMANS 8:25

294
*Live and work without pride. Be gentle
and kind. Do not be hard on others.
Let love keep you from doing that.*
EPHESIANS 4:2

295
*Rest in the Lord and be willing to wait for Him.
Do not trouble yourself when all goes well with
the one who carries out his sinful plans.*
PSALM 37:7

296
But they who wait upon the Lord will get new strength. They will rise up with wings like eagles. They will run and not get tired. They will walk and not become weak.
Isaiah 40:31

297
The Lord is good to those who wait for Him, to the one who looks for Him.
Lamentations 3:25

298
I did not give up waiting for the Lord. And He turned to me and heard my cry.
Psalm 40:1

299
*You must be willing to wait also.
Be strong in your hearts because
the Lord is coming again soon.*
JAMES 5:8

300
*Christian brothers, be willing to wait for
the Lord to come again. Learn from the
farmer. He waits for the good fruit from the
earth until the early and late rains come.*
JAMES 5:7

⋛ PEACE ⋚

God wants you to have peace in your heart. You might say, "Wow! Does He know what I'm going through? Peace feels impossible with all the stuff I'm facing." But peace *is* possible, even in the middle of life's storms. Troubles will come, yes. But if you walk closely with Jesus—if you don't take your eyes off Him—God promises to bless you with supernatural peace. So, keep your thoughts on Him, no matter what!

301
"I have told you these things so you may have peace in Me. In the world you will have much trouble. But take hope! I have power over the world!"
JOHN 16:33

302
May the Lord of peace give you His peace at all times. The Lord be with you all.
2 THESSALONIANS 3:16

303
"You will keep the man in perfect peace whose mind is kept on You, because he trusts in You."
Isaiah 26:3

304
"Those who make peace are happy, because they will be called the sons of God."
Matthew 5:9

305
"Peace I leave with you. My peace I give to you. I do not give peace to you as the world gives. Do not let your hearts be troubled or afraid."
John 14:27

306
Let the peace of Christ have power over your hearts. You were chosen as a part of His body. Always be thankful.
Colossians 3:15

307

Be at peace with all men. Live a holy life. No one will see the Lord without having that kind of life.
HEBREWS 12:14

308

As much as you can, live in peace with all men.
ROMANS 12:18

309

I will lie down and sleep in peace. O Lord, You alone keep me safe.
PSALM 4:8

310

Turn away from what is sinful. Do what is good. Look for peace and go after it.
1 PETER 3:11

⋛ PRAYER ⋚

What if talking to God could be as natural and comfortable as talking to a good friend? It should be! The Lord wants you to spend time telling Him all you're going through—the good and the bad. He wants to be the first person you run to when you're hurting, and the first person you tell your good news. And remember, prayer is not a one-way conversation. If you listen closely, God is speaking to your heart too!

311

Do not worry. Learn to pray about everything. Give thanks to God as you ask Him for what you need.
PHILIPPIANS 4:6

312

"Because of this, I say to you, whatever you ask for when you pray, have faith that you will receive it. Then you will get it."
MARK 11:24

313

*Jesus told them a picture-story
to show that men should always
pray and not give up.*
LUKE 18:1

314

*"When you pray, go into a room by yourself.
After you have shut the door, pray to your
Father Who is in secret. Then your Father
Who sees in secret will reward you."*
MATTHEW 6:6

315

*Tell your sins to each other. And pray for each
other so you may be healed. The prayer from the
heart of a man right with God has much power.*
JAMES 5:16

316

*"Call to Me, and I will answer you.
And I will show you great and wonderful
things which you do not know."*
JEREMIAH 33:3

317
Never stop praying.
1 Thessalonians 5:17

318
"Pray like this: 'Our Father in heaven, Your name is holy. May Your holy nation come. What You want done, may it be done on earth as it is in heaven.' "
Matthew 6:9–10

319
In the same way, the Holy Spirit helps us where we are weak. We do not know how to pray or what we should pray for, but the Holy Spirit prays to God for us with sounds that cannot be put into words.
Romans 8:26

320
I want men everywhere to pray. They should lift up holy hands as they pray. They should not be angry or argue.
1 Timothy 2:8

PRIDE HAS TO GO!

Have you ever met someone who's prideful? Maybe he thinks he's the smartest kid in school. Maybe he thinks all the girls will like him best because he's so handsome. God isn't a big fan of pride. In fact, His Word says that pride leads to a fall. Watch out if you start bragging on yourself! You might just take a tumble! Instead of singing your own praises, praise God and others. As you lift them up, God will lift you up! What an awesome promise!

321
When pride comes, then comes shame, but wisdom is with those who have no pride.
PROVERBS 11:2

322
Pride comes before being destroyed and a proud spirit comes before a fall.
PROVERBS 16:18

323
A man's pride will bring him down, but he whose spirit is without pride will receive honor.
PROVERBS 29:23

324
If anyone thinks he is important when he is nothing, he is fooling himself.
GALATIANS 6:3

325
Do not love the world or anything in the world. If anyone loves the world, the Father's love is not in him. For everything that is in the world does not come from the Father. The desires of our flesh and the things our eyes see and want and the pride of this life come from the world.
1 JOHN 2:15–16

326
Live in peace with each other. Do not act or think with pride. Be happy to be with poor people. Keep yourself from thinking you are so wise.
ROMANS 12:16

327

But He gives us more loving-favor. For the Holy Writings say, "God works against the proud but gives loving-favor to those who have no pride."
JAMES 4:6

328

Nothing should be done because of pride or thinking about yourself. Think of other people as more important than yourself.
PHILIPPIANS 2:3

329

Let another man praise you, and not your own mouth. Let a stranger, and not your own lips.
PROVERBS 27:2

330

Eyes lifted high and a proud heart is sin and is the lamp of the sinful.
PROVERBS 21:4

⇒ PROBLEMS ⇐

Have you ever wished you could live a problem-free life? Things would be much easier if you didn't have so many bumps in the road. But think about it like this: problems are great opportunities to learn life's lessons. If you never had problems, God wouldn't have to come up with solutions! He wants to prove that He's bigger than anything you might face, so don't panic when troubles come. He promises to give an answer!

331
Those who are right with the Lord cry, and He hears them. And He takes them from all their troubles.
PSALM 34:17

332
The man who does not give up when tests come is happy. After the test is over, he will receive the crown of life. God has promised this to those who love Him.
JAMES 1:12

333
"I have told you these things so you may have peace in Me. In the world you will have much trouble. But take hope! I have power over the world!"
JOHN 16:33

334
But the Lord knows how to help men who are right with God when they are tempted. He also knows how to keep the sinners suffering for their wrong-doing until the day they stand before God Who will judge them.
2 PETER 2:9

335
He who watches over his mouth and his tongue keeps his soul from troubles.
PROVERBS 21:23

336
The one who is right with God is kept from trouble, but the sinful get into trouble instead.
PROVERBS 11:8

337
We know that God makes all things work together for the good of those who love Him and are chosen to be a part of His plan.
ROMANS 8:28

338
Our hope comes from God. May He fill you with joy and peace because of your trust in Him. May your hope grow stronger by the power of the Holy Spirit.
ROMANS 15:13

339

*After you have suffered for awhile,
God Himself will make you perfect. He will
keep you in the right way. He will give you
strength. He is the God of all loving-favor
and has called you through Christ Jesus
to share His shining-greatness forever.*
1 PETER 5:10

340

*"Do not fear, for I am with you. Do not be afraid,
for I am your God. I will give you strength, and
for sure I will help you. Yes, I will hold you up
with My right hand that is right and good."*
ISAIAH 41:10

RUN THE RACE

Have you ever run a race? When you start, it seems like so much fun. You're absolutely sure you can make it all the way to the finish line. But, as you run, you start to get out of breath. Your legs feel funny. You get thirsty. You wonder if you'll make it to the end. Life is a lot like a race. God wants you to keep going— even when you don't feel like it. When you do what His Word says, He promises you'll take the prize at the end!

341
You know that only one person gets a crown for being in a race even if many people run. You must run so you will win the crown.
1 CORINTHIANS 9:24

342
I have fought a good fight. I have finished the work I was to do. I have kept the faith.
2 TIMOTHY 4:7

343

*I will run the way of Your Law,
for You will give me a willing heart.*
PSALM 119:32

344

No, Christian brothers, I do not have that life yet. But I do one thing. I forget everything that is behind me and look forward to that which is ahead of me. My eyes are on the crown. I want to win the race and get the crown of God's call from heaven through Christ Jesus.
PHILIPPIANS 3:13–14

345

*You were doing well. Who stopped
you from obeying the truth?*
GALATIANS 5:7

346
All these many people who have had faith in God are around us like a cloud. Let us put every thing out of our lives that keeps us from doing what we should. Let us keep running in the race that God has planned for us.
HEBREWS 12:1

347
"But the one who stays true to the end will be saved."
MATTHEW 24:13

348
You must be willing to wait without giving up. After you have done what God wants you to do, God will give you what He promised you.
HEBREWS 10:36

349

Those who have Christian owners must respect their owners because they are Christian brothers. They should work hard for them because much-loved Christian brothers are being helped by their work. Teach and preach these things.
1 TIMOTHY 6:2

350

Anyone who runs in a race must follow the rules to get the crown.
2 TIMOTHY 2:5

⋛ SCHOOL DAYS ⋚

From the day you're born, you're always learning. You learn how to eat, how to walk, and how to talk. As you get older and go to school, you learn all sorts of things—math, science, geography, and much more. You learn how to sit still and pay attention and how to treat adults with respect. God loves it that you're a willing learner. He's got so much more to teach you as life goes on.
Will you be a happy student?

351
A wise man will hear and grow in learning. A man of understanding will become able to understand a saying.
PROVERBS 1:5–6

352
The fear of the Lord is the beginning of much learning. Fools hate wisdom and teaching.
PROVERBS 1:7

353
An understanding mind gets much learning, and the ear of the wise listens for much learning.
PROVERBS 18:15

354
Give teaching to a wise man and he will be even wiser. Teach a man who is right and good, and he will grow in learning.
PROVERBS 9:9

355
Keep on doing all the things you learned and received and heard from me. Do the things you saw me do. Then the God Who gives peace will be with you.
PHILIPPIANS 4:9

356
You must teach what is right and true.
TITUS 2:1

357

All the Holy Writings are God-given and are made alive by Him. Man is helped when he is taught God's Word. It shows what is wrong. It changes the way of a man's life. It shows him how to be right with God.
2 TIMOTHY 3:16

358

I will show you and teach you in the way you should go. I will tell you what to do with My eye upon you.
PSALM 32:8

359

Jesus grew strong in mind and body. He grew in favor with God and men.
LUKE 2:52

360

"The Helper is the Holy Spirit. The Father will send Him in My place. He will teach you everything and help you remember everything I have told you."
JOHN 14:26

SELF-CONTROL

Control yourself! Maybe you've heard your mom speak those words. Oh, but it's hard to control yourself—especially if you're upset. It's also hard when you're tempted to do the wrong thing—like eat the whole cake instead of just one slice. It takes a lot of self-control to say no to your own desires and wishes, but the Lord really wants you to do your very best, brave boy. And don't worry! The Holy Spirit will help you, if you just ask. That's a promise!

361
A man who cannot rule his own spirit is like a city whose walls are broken down.
PROVERBS 25:28

362
Older men are to be quiet and to be careful how they act. They are to be the boss over their own desires. Their faith and love are to stay strong and they are not to give up.
TITUS 2:2

363

But the fruit that comes from having the Holy Spirit in our lives is: love, joy, peace, not giving up, being kind, being good, having faith, being gentle, and being the boss over our own desires. The Law is not against these things.
GALATIANS 5:22–23

364

*The end of the world is near.
You must be the boss over your mind.
Keep awake so you can pray.*
1 PETER 4:7

365

He who is slow to anger is better than the powerful. And he who rules his spirit is better than he who takes a city.
PROVERBS 16:32

366

He must like to take people into his home. He must love what is good. He must be able to think well and do all things in the right way. He must live a holy life and be the boss over his own desires.
TITUS 1:8

367

O Lord, put a watch over my mouth.
Keep watch over the door of my lips.
PSALM 141:3

368

As you have a better understanding, be able to say no when you need to. Do not give up. And as you wait and do not give up, live God-like.
2 PETER 1:6

369

We are taught to have nothing to do with that which is against God. We are to have nothing to do with the desires of this world. We are to be wise and to be right with God. We are to live God-like lives in this world.
TITUS 2:12

370

A fool always loses his temper,
but a wise man keeps quiet.
PROVERBS 29:11

SERVING OTHERS

God has called you to be a servant. You might be thinking, *Wait a minute! Am I supposed to be everyone's waiter or cleaner? How far does this servant thing go?* The truth is this: serving and loving go hand in hand. When you love someone, you want to care for them and make sure they have what they need. So don't chase after money or things. Don't be selfish. Live to serve others and you'll please God's heart.

371

"For the Son of Man did not come to be cared for. He came to care for others. He came to give His life so that many could be bought by His blood and be made free from sin."
MARK 10:45

372

God has given each of you a gift. Use it to help each other. This will show God's loving-favor.
1 PETER 4:10

373

"If you think it is wrong to serve the Lord, choose today whom you will serve. Choose the gods your fathers worshiped on the other side of the river, or choose the gods of the Amorites in whose land you are living. But as for me and my family, we will serve the Lord."
JOSHUA 24:15

374

Christian brother, you were chosen to be free. Be careful that you do not please your old selves by sinning because you are free. Live this free life by loving and helping others.
GALATIANS 5:13

375

"He who is greatest among you will be the one to care for you."
MATTHEW 23:11

376

Jesus sat down and called the followers to Him. He said, "If anyone wants to be first, he must be last of all. He will be the one to care for all."
MARK 9:35

377

"No one can have two bosses. He will hate the one and love the other. Or he will listen to the one and work against the other. You cannot have both God and riches as your boss at the same time."
MATTHEW 6:24

378

You obey the whole Law when you do this one thing, "Love your neighbor as you love yourself."
GALATIANS 5:14

379
God always does what is right. He will not forget the work you did to help the Christians and the work you are still doing to help them. This shows your love for Christ.
HEBREWS 6:10

380
"Follow the Lord your God and fear Him. Keep His Laws, and listen to His voice. Work for Him, and hold on to Him."
DEUTERONOMY 13:4

SNEAKY BEHAVIOR

Some kids are so sneaky! When their parents or teachers are around, they pretend to be doing the right thing; but as soon as the grown-ups aren't watching, the truth comes out. God wants you to be who you say you are. What you do in secret is just as important—maybe even more so—as what you do in the sight of others. Are you who you say you are—or are you just sneaking around?

381
It will not go well for the man who hides his sins, but he who tells his sins and turns from them will be given loving-pity.
PROVERBS 28:13

382
Jesus said to them, "You are the kind of people who make yourselves look good before other people. God knows your hearts. What men think is good is hated in the eyes of God."
LUKE 16:15

383

"You who pretend to be someone you are not, first take the big piece of wood out of your own eye. Then you can see better to take the small piece of wood out of your brother's eye."
MATTHEW 7:5

384

"For there is nothing covered up that will not be seen. There is nothing hidden that will not be known."
LUKE 12:2

385

If we say we are joined together with Him but live in darkness, we are telling a lie. We are not living the truth.
1 JOHN 1:6

386

"Not everyone who says to me, 'Lord, Lord,' will go into the holy nation of heaven. The one who does the things My Father in heaven wants him to do will go into the holy nation of heaven."
MATTHEW 7:21

387

He whose ways are false will not live in my house. He who tells lies will not stand in front of me.
PSALM 101:7

388

They say they know God, but by the way they act, they show that they do not. They are sinful people. They will not obey and are of no use for any good work.
TITUS 1:16

389

"The heart is fooled more than anything else, and is very sinful. Who can know how bad it is?"
JEREMIAH 17:9

390

Anyone who says, "I know Him," but does not obey His teaching is a liar. There is no truth in him.
1 JOHN 2:4

⋛ SPORTS ⋚

Are you into sports? If so, do you like to win? Winning is fun, but you know what's even more fun? Being a good sport. Even if you're really good at what you do, you don't ever want to think more highly of yourself than others. So, go ahead and play the game, but keep the bigger prize in mind—honoring God. When you do that, He promises to help you. . .not only in this life, but in the life to come.

391

Anyone who runs in a race must follow the rules to get the crown.
2 TIMOTHY 2:5

392

Growing strong in body is all right but growing in God-like living is more important. It will not only help you in this life now but in the next life also.
1 TIMOTHY 4:8

393

*Let another man praise you,
and not your own mouth. Let a
stranger, and not your own lips.*
PROVERBS 27:2

394

*Pride comes before being destroyed
and a proud spirit comes before a fall.*
PROVERBS 16:18

395

*My eyes are on the crown. I want to
win the race and get the crown of God's
call from heaven through Christ Jesus.*
PHILIPPIANS 3:14

396

*"The person who thinks he is important
will find out how little he is worth.
The person who is not trying to honor
himself will be made important."*
MATTHEW 23:12

397
*I can do all things because
Christ gives me the strength.*
PHILIPPIANS 4:13

398
*Do not be full of joy when the one who hates you
falls. Do not let your heart be glad when he trips.
The Lord will see it and will not be pleased, and
He will turn away His anger from him.*
PROVERBS 24:17–18

399
*Nothing should be done because of pride
or thinking about yourself. Think of other
people as more important than yourself.*
PHILIPPIANS 2:3

400
*He will make you strong with power in
your hearts through the Holy Spirit.*
EPHESIANS 3:16

STAND STRONG

There are going to be days when you feel so weak that standing strong seems impossible. You'll just want to crawl into bed and pull the covers over your head. But even on those days, when things are really, really tough, God wants you to stand strong. Remember, it's His strength, not yours. So you can rest easy in Him! That's a promise guaranteed to make you feel better.

401
Stand against him and be strong in your faith. Remember, other Christians over all the world are suffering the same as you are.
1 Peter 5:9

402
Watch and keep awake! Stand true to the Lord. Keep on acting like men and be strong.
1 Corinthians 16:13

403
So lift up your hands that have been weak. Stand up on your weak legs.
Hebrews 12:12

404
There is One Who can keep you from falling and can bring you before Himself free from all sin. He can give you great joy as you stand before Him in His shining-greatness.
Jude 1:24

405
Because of this, put on all the things God gives you to fight with. Then you will be able to stand in that sinful day. When it is all over, you will still be standing.
Ephesians 6:13

406

Dear friends, if our heart does not say that we are wrong, we will have no fear as we stand before Him.
1 JOHN 3:21

407

This is the last thing I want to say: Be strong with the Lord's strength.
EPHESIANS 6:10

408

Live your lives as the Good News of Christ says you should. If I come to you or not, I want to hear that you are standing true as one. I want to hear that you are working together as one, preaching the Good News.
PHILIPPIANS 1:27

409
*So stand up and do not be moved.
Wear a belt of truth around your
body. Wear a piece of iron over your
chest which is being right with God.*
EPHESIANS 6:14

410
*So give yourselves to God. Stand against the
devil and he will run away from you.*
JAMES 4:7

STICKY SITUATIONS

Have you ever been tempted to do the wrong thing? Sure, everyone has! Some kids are tempted to cheat on a test. Others are tempted to eat junk food too much. Still others are tempted to hang out with kids who are bad influences. Jesus understands temptation. He was tempted by the devil. But guess what? He didn't give in to temptation. He has shown us that we don't have to give in either!

411

You have never been tempted to sin in any different way than other people. God is faithful. He will not allow you to be tempted more than you can take. But when you are tempted, He will make a way for you to keep from falling into sin.
1 CORINTHIANS 10:13

412

"Watch and pray so that you will not be tempted. Man's spirit wants to do this, but the body does not have the power to do it."
MARK 14:38

413

Christian brothers, if a person is found doing some sin, you who are stronger Christians should lead that one back into the right way. Do not be proud as you do it. Watch yourself, because you may be tempted also.
GALATIANS 6:1

414

Even when we were with you, we told you that much trouble would come to us. It has come as you can see. . . . I was afraid the devil had tempted you.
1 THESSALONIANS 3:4–5

415

When you are tempted to do wrong, do not say, "God is tempting me." God cannot be tempted. He will never tempt anyone.
JAMES 1:13

416

Because Jesus was tempted as we are and suffered as we do, He understands us and He is able to help us when we are tempted.
HEBREWS 2:18

417

A man is tempted to do wrong when he lets himself be led by what his bad thoughts tell him to do.
JAMES 1:14

418

But the Lord knows how to help men who are right with God when they are tempted. He also knows how to keep the sinners suffering for their wrong-doing until the day they stand before God Who will judge them.
2 PETER 2:9

419
*Jesus was led by the Holy Spirit to a desert.
There He was tempted by the devil.*
MATTHEW 4:1

420
*A man who hurts people tempts his
neighbor to do the same, and leads
him in a way that is not good.*
PROVERBS 16:29

⸔ SUPERHEROES ⸕

Maybe you're like a lot of boys who enjoy watching superhero movies. Maybe you even collect the action figures. There's one superhero who's greater than any superhero you've ever seen on the big screen—Jesus! You can read about Him in His Word, the Bible, and learn how He wants to grow you into a superhero too. You won't leap from building to building with a single bound, but—with His help—you *can* change the world.

421

"Learn to do good. Look for what is right and fair. Speak strong words to those who make it hard for people. Stand up for the rights of those who have no parents. Help the woman whose husband has died."
ISAIAH 1:17

422

This is the last thing I want to say: Be strong with the Lord's strength.
EPHESIANS 6:10

423

"Have I not told you? Be strong and have strength of heart! Do not be afraid or lose faith. For the Lord your God is with you anywhere you go."
JOSHUA 1:9

424

Who will rise up for me against the sinful? Who will take a stand for me against those who do wrong?
PSALM 94:16

425

The holy nation of God is not made up of words. It is made up of power.
1 CORINTHIANS 4:20

426

But they who wait upon the Lord will get new strength. They will rise up with wings like eagles. They will run and not get tired. They will walk and not become weak.
ISAIAH 40:31

427

*For God did not give us a spirit of fear.
He gave us a spirit of power and
of love and of a good mind.*
2 Timothy 1:7

428

*"Do not fear, for I am with you. Do not be afraid,
for I am your God. I will give you strength, and
for sure I will help you. Yes, I will hold you up
with My right hand that is right and good."*
Isaiah 41:10

429

*From the beginning of the world, men could
see what God is like through the things
He has made. This shows His power that
lasts forever. It shows that He is God.*
Romans 1:20

430

*"For the Lord your God is the One Who
goes with you. He will fight for you against
those who hate you. And He will save you."*
Deuteronomy 20:4

⇒ THIS IS A TEST ⇐

How do you feel about tests? Do you panic when you sit down to answer all those questions? Or are you calm and collected? Tests in school are unavoidable. But so are "life tests." Challenges will come, and your beliefs will be tested. . .but God wants you to be faithful no matter what happens. The Bible promises if you come through the fiery trials and remain faithful, you'll be pure as gold or silver.

431

These tests have come to prove your faith and to show that it is good. Gold, which can be destroyed, is tested by fire. Your faith is worth much more than gold and it must be tested also. Then your faith will bring thanks and shining-greatness and honor to Jesus Christ when He comes again.
1 PETER 1:7

432

"Will it be well when He tests you? Or do you lie to Him as one lies to a man?"
JOB 13:9

433
God has allowed us to be trusted with the Good News. Because of this, we preach it to please God, not man. God tests and proves our hearts.
1 Thessalonians 2:4

434
Dear friends, your faith is going to be tested as if it were going through fire. Do not be surprised at this. Be happy that you are able to share some of the suffering of Christ. When His shining-greatness is shown, you will be filled with much joy.
1 Peter 4:12–13

435
The melting-pot is for silver and the hot fire is for gold, but the Lord tests hearts.
Proverbs 17:3

436
The man who does not give up when tests come is happy. After the test is over, he will receive the crown of life. God has promised this to those who love Him.
James 1:12

437

My Christian brothers, you should be happy when you have all kinds of tests.
JAMES 1:2

438

With this hope you can be happy even if you need to have sorrow and all kinds of tests for awhile.
1 PETER 1:6

439

Let the sins of the sinful stop. But build up those who are right with You. For the God Who is right and good tests both the hearts and the minds.
PSALM 7:9

440

The Lord is in His holy house. The Lord's throne is in heaven. His eyes see as He tests the sons of men.
PSALM 11:4

TRUSTING GOD

What does it mean to put your trust in someone? It means you're counting on them to do what they say. You hope they won't let you down. Unfortunately, people do let us down from time to time—it's part of being human. (Hey, even you have let people down a few times. . .right?) Would you like to know someone who will never let you down? You already do—it's Jesus! You can put all your trust in Him, and He will never break your heart. That's the best promise ever!

441
He will not be afraid of bad news. His heart is strong because he trusts in the Lord.
PSALM 112:7

442
Those who know Your name will put their trust in You. For You, O Lord, have never left alone those who look for You.
PSALM 9:10

443

*The Lord is my strength and my safe cover.
My heart trusts in Him, and I am helped. So my
heart is full of joy. I will thank Him with my song.*
PSALM 28:7

444

*Trust in the Lord with all your heart,
and do not trust in your own understanding.*
PROVERBS 3:5

445

*"You will keep the man in perfect peace whose
mind is kept on You, because he trusts in You."*
ISAIAH 26:3

446

*[Jesus] said to her, "Daughter,
your faith has healed you. Go in
peace and be free from your sickness."*
MARK 5:34

447
*It is better to trust in the
Lord than to trust in man.*
Psalm 118:8

448
*Give your way over to the Lord.
Trust in Him also. And He will do it.*
Psalm 37:5

449
*"Good will come to the man who trusts
in the Lord, and whose hope is in the Lord.
He will be like a tree planted by the water,
that sends out its roots by the river. It will
not be afraid when the heat comes but its
leaves will be green. It will not be troubled
in a dry year, or stop giving fruit."*
Jeremiah 17:7–8

450
When I am afraid, I will trust in You.
Psalm 56:3

WATCH THOSE WORDS!

What you say is important—whether you're talking to your friends, your parents, or your teachers. They care not only about what you say, but how you say it. Sure, sometimes you say the wrong thing. You get angry. You smart off. But Jesus wants you to speak the way He does—with love, compassion, and truth. Keep a close eye on your words, brave boy! They say a lot about who you are and who you serve.

451

Watch your talk! No bad words should be coming from your mouth. Say what is good. Your words should help others grow as Christians.
EPHESIANS 4:29

452

O Lord, put a watch over my mouth. Keep watch over the door of my lips.
PSALM 141:3

453

*My mouth will speak wisdom. And the thoughts
of my heart will be understanding.*
PSALM 49:3

454

*Death and life are in the power of the tongue,
and those who love it will eat its fruit.*
PROVERBS 18:21

455

*My Christian brothers, you know everyone
should listen much and speak little.
He should be slow to become angry.*
JAMES 1:19

456

*A gentle answer turns away anger,
but a sharp word causes anger.*
PROVERBS 15:1

457

With our tongue we give thanks to our Father in heaven. And with our tongue we speak bad words against men who are made like God. Giving thanks and speaking bad words come from the same mouth. My Christian brothers, this is not right!
JAMES 3:9–10

458

He who watches over his mouth and his tongue keeps his soul from troubles.
PROVERBS 21:23

459

Pleasing words are like honey. They are sweet to the soul and healing to the bones.
PROVERBS 16:24

460

A gentle tongue is a tree of life, but a sinful tongue crushes the spirit.
PROVERBS 15:4

WISE BEYOND YOUR YEARS

Are wisdom and knowledge the same thing? Maybe you're book smart, and you make straight A's. Does that make you wise? Here's the truth: wisdom is God knowledge. This means you can't learn it in books. However, you can get it from hanging out with Jesus and learning to live the way He wants you to. So, here's the very best thing you can do: obtain knowledge (study your lessons) but get wisdom (from God and His Word) too. God promises to give it if you ask.

461

If you do not have wisdom, ask God for it. He is always ready to give it to you and will never say you are wrong for asking.
JAMES 1:5

462

For the Lord gives wisdom. Much learning and understanding come from His mouth.
PROVERBS 2:6

463

*Happy is the man who finds wisdom,
and the man who gets understanding. For
it is better than getting silver and fine gold.*
PROVERBS 3:13–14

464

*Listen to words about what you should do,
and take your punishment if you need it,
so that you may be wise the rest of your days.*
PROVERBS 19:20

465

*The way of a fool is right in his own eyes,
but a wise man listens to good teaching.*
PROVERBS 12:15

466

*"For I will give you wisdom in what to
say and I will help you say it. Those who
are against you will not be able to stop
you or say you are wrong."*
LUKE 21:15

467

The fear of the Lord is the beginning of much learning. Fools hate wisdom and teaching.
PROVERBS 1:7

468

The fear of the Lord is the beginning of wisdom. To learn about the Holy One is understanding.
PROVERBS 9:10

469

The beginning of wisdom is: Get wisdom! And with all you have gotten, get understanding.
PROVERBS 4:7

470

"Whoever hears these words of Mine and does them, will be like a wise man who built his house on rock."
MATTHEW 7:24

WITNESSING FOR CHRIST

If you discovered a medicine that would cure the deadliest disease, would you tell people about it? If you found a million dollars in a field, would you share the news with those you love? Sure you would! When you have exciting news to tell, you don't hold anything back. Here's a fun fact: you already have the best news there is! Jesus is the Savior of the world. Don't hold back. Let everyone know!

471
"Let your light shine in front of men. Then they will see the good things you do and will honor your Father Who is in heaven."
MATTHEW 5:16

472
"But you will receive power when the Holy Spirit comes into your life. You will tell about Me in the city of Jerusalem and over all the countries of Judea and Samaria and to the ends of the earth."
ACTS 1:8

473

Then I heard the voice of the Lord, saying, "Whom should I send? Who will go for Us?" Then I said, "Here am I. Send me!"
ISAIAH 6:8

474

I am not ashamed of the Good News. It is the power of God. It is the way He saves men from the punishment of their sins if they put their trust in Him. It is for the Jew first and for all other people also.
ROMANS 1:16

475

He put a new song in my mouth, a song of praise to our God. Many will see and fear and will put their trust in the Lord.
PSALM 40:3

476

Do not be ashamed to tell others about what our Lord said, or of me here in prison. I am here because of Jesus Christ. Be ready to suffer for preaching the Good News and God will give you the strength you need.
2 Timothy 1:8

477

"And when I am lifted up from the earth, I will attract all people toward Me."
John 12:3

478

"Go and make followers of all the nations. Baptize them in the name of the Father and of the Son and of the Holy Spirit. Teach them to do all the things I have told you. And I am with you always, even to the end of the world."
Matthew 28:19–20

479

*"You can speak for Me," says the Lord.
"You are My servant whom I have chosen
so that you may know and believe Me, and
understand that I am He. No God was made
before Me, and there will be none after Me."*
ISAIAH 43:10

480

*"This Good News about the holy
nation of God must be preached
over all the earth. It must be told to
all nations and then the end will come."*
MATTHEW 24:14

WORRY GETS YOU NOWHERE

When you're worried, who do you talk to? Jesus promises to take your worries if you'll just give them to Him. No matter what you're upset about—your grades, a friendship, or your relationship with your parents—you can go straight to Him. The Lord promises to take those worries and give you the faith you need to get through the situation. All you need to do is pray and ask Him to help you. And in that moment, His peace will flood over you.

481

Do not worry. Learn to pray about everything. Give thanks to God as you ask Him for what you need. The peace of God is much greater than the human mind can understand. This peace will keep your hearts and minds through Christ Jesus.
PHILIPPIANS 4:6–7

482
*Give all your worries to Him
because He cares for you.*
1 Peter 5:7

483
*"I tell you this: Do not worry about
your life. Do not worry about what you
are going to eat and drink. Do not worry
about what you are going to wear. Is not
life more important than food? Is not
the body more important than clothes?"*
Matthew 6:25

484
*Worry in the heart of a man weighs
it down, but a good word makes it glad.*
Proverbs 12:25

485
"Do not worry about tomorrow. Tomorrow will have its own worries. The troubles we have in a day are enough for one day."
MATTHEW 6:34

486
"Peace I leave with you. My peace I give to you. I do not give peace to you as the world gives. Do not let your hearts be troubled or afraid."
JOHN 14:27

487
Give all your cares to the Lord and He will give you strength. He will never let those who are right with Him be shaken.
PSALM 55:22

488
*"Do not let your heart be troubled.
You have put your trust in God,
put your trust in Me also."*
JOHN 14:1

489
*"Which of you can make yourself
a little taller by worrying?"*
LUKE 12:25

490
*Jesus said to His followers, "Because of this,
I say to you, do not worry about your life,
what you are going to eat. Do not worry about
your body, what you are going to wear."*
LUKE 12:22

YOU'RE THE ONLY BOY LIKE YOU

There's no one on planet Earth just like you. No one has your smile, your hair, your fingerprint, or your exact personality. You are truly one-of-a-kind, brave boy! And God wants you to celebrate your uniqueness. Don't worry about fitting in, no matter how hard your friends beg. Don't try to be like anyone else. You just be you. . .and enjoy every moment!

491

I will give thanks to You, for the greatness of the way I was made brings fear. Your works are great and my soul knows it very well.
PSALM 139:14

492

"Before I started to put you together in your mother, I knew you. Before you were born, I set you apart as holy. I chose you to speak to the nations for Me."
JEREMIAH 1:5

493

We are His work. He has made us to belong to Christ Jesus so we can work for Him. He planned that we should do this.
Ephesians 2:10

494

"God knows how many hairs you have on your head."
Matthew 10:30

495

" 'For I know the plans I have for you,' says the Lord, 'plans for well-being and not for trouble, to give you a future and a hope.' "
Jeremiah 29:11

496
*But now, O Lord, You are our Father.
We are the clay, and You are our pot maker.
All of us are the work of Your hand.*
ISAIAH 64:8

497
*For You made the parts inside me.
You put me together inside my mother.*
PSALM 139:13

498
*There are many people who belong to Christ.
And yet, we are one body which is Christ's. We
are all different but we depend on each other.*
ROMANS 12:5

499

*The Holy Spirit has been given
to you and you all know the truth.*
1 JOHN 2:20

500

*But the Lord said to Samuel, "Do not look
at the way he looks on the outside or how
tall he is, because I have not chosen him.
For the Lord does not look at the things man
looks at. A man looks at the outside of a
person, but the Lord looks at the heart."*
1 SAMUEL 16:7

MORE GREAT RESOURCES FOR BRAVE BOYS!

Choose Adventure

You will be encouraged to live an adventurous life for God with these 180 devotions and prayers. Each just-right-sized reading will challenge you to be brave in the faith like dozens of Bible heroes including David, Daniel, Paul, Noah, Joseph, and more—while you come to know and understand how you can be brave too!

Paperback / 978-1-64352-802-1 / $4.99

A to Z Devotions Brave Boys

What makes a brave boy of God? . . . You will discover the answers in this delightful A to Z devotional! *A to Z Devotions for Brave Boys* introduces you to a positive character trait for every letter of the alphabet alongside an inspiring devotional reading.

Hardback / 978-1-64352-515-0 / $14.99

With your parent's permission, check out ForBraveBoys.com where you'll discover additional positive faith-building activites and resources!